INTRODUCTION

Of the many species of birds that may be kept within the confines of your home or garden, finches are undoubtedly the most popular for numerous reasons. Being small, they do not consume high quantities of food, they are very quiet, they are not destructive to their accommodation, and, for many any of a number of small seed eating birds, also referred to as hardbills. The distinction between seed eaters, or hardbills, and softbilled birds (those whose diet is predominately of a soft nature— fruits, insects and the like), is by no means clear-cut. Many species regarded as being finch-like may consume large

Being small, finches and finch-like birds are relatively easy to cater to, are not destructive to their accommodation, and are considerably less expensive than parrots or larger birds.

species, they are less costly to purchase than parrots or softbilled birds. Cared for in the correct manner, many finches may live for ten or more years, and quite a large number of species have proven to be excellent breeding birds under captive conditions.

In avicultural terms, a finch is quantities of soft foods, especially during their breeding season, so you should never assume that your finch will be properly satisfied with a seed-only diet.

As aviary birds, finches are delightful occupants. Many have sweet, if not especially, melodious voices, and many are extremely colorful. By nature they are gregarious birds, so are always best kept in pairs, and invariably in small family or mixed collection groups. Some species, such as Canaries, Zebra Finches, and Gouldian Finches, have been bred in such numbers that they are now regarded as domesticated. They are seen in a wide range of colors, and are very popular exhibition birds. Other species are quite costly, comparatively rare, and not easily bred in captivity.

In this book all aspects of selection and management are detailed in order that the first time owner can maintain, and maybe breed, a small collection of these birds. All of the very popular species seen in aviculture are described in the species section, as well as a few that are regarded as difficult for the novice, but worthy of those wishing to be more specialized in their endeavors. Keeping finch and finch-like birds is a most rewarding pastime that can be enjoyed by the whole family. It is an especially relaxing hobby in a world in which this is a most beneficial way of unwinding from the hectic pace of modern society.

By nature finches are gregarious birds, and are therefore best kept in pairs or in mixed collection groups. Here the Owl Finch *(Poephila bichenovi)* is comfortably at home with a group of Long-Tailed Finches *(Poephila acuticauda acuticauda)*.

SELECTING THE RIGHT SPECIES

If you have never kept birds before there are a few important facts that should be considered before you go out and start purchasing stock.

WHY ARE THE BIRDS WANTED?

There are many reasons why you may wish to keep finches and these will influence the choice of stock, and where to purchase it from. If you plan to show your birds, then you will need to obtain stock from a well-established breeder of exhibition stock. It is better to commence with such birds rather than simply exhibit exotic finches which may not have a good captive breeding record. If you simply want to have a mixed collection of finches in an ornamental aviary (which may be of the indoor or outdoor type), these can be purchased from pet stores. In a mixed collection aviary, the chances of breeding success will be rather less than if you allocate large indoor cages or separate aviaries for either single species groups, or pairs. When breeding single species groups, you are more able to cater to the specific needs of the birds.

If you wish to become a finch breeder, then it is always wiser to restrict the species you keep to only one or two, and then really devote all of your efforts to just these. If you have the space and the cash, you could always have an ornamental aviary as well as a sideline to your main pursuit. If you are interested in breeding your finches, visit your local pet store, which should be an excellent source of information on the subject.

Green Singing Finch (*Serinus mozam-bicus*). Though not as colorful as the waxbills, the Green Singing Finch seldom fails to attract attention because of its bright yellow underparts and cheerful little song.

COMPATIBILITY

When selecting birds for a mixed collection it is important that you bear a few crucial facts in mind, especially if you plan to hang up nest boxes for all or some of the species. Birds, like people, do not always get on well with each other, the more so if the accommodation is crowded. It is not possible to say that this or that species will not get on with another species because there are so many aspects that will influence compatibility. However, certain general facts are applicable to all species.

During the breeding season, most species will become far more aggressive than in the non-breeding period. They will be more territorial, and will not tolerate other birds nesting or even perching near their nest. The result is that some species will be much more dominant than others, so the more timid species will be constantly in a fearful state. As a guide, never try to mix birds of differing sizes together until you have gained experience on the whole matter of avian compatibility.

Birds which exhibit similar plumage colors will tend to squabble more than those of dissimilar colors. Unpaired hens will invariably be a source of trouble, for they will attack the chicks of established hens, or prove a nuisance by trying to help a hen rear her chicks!

The number of available perches in an aviary, as well as the number and location of food stations, are other factors that will determine how well a given collection of birds will get on with each other. The golden rule is to always strive for a situation that allows each bird (or pair), to have sufficient room to itself, and enough places of refuge for it to retreat to, should it feel the need for this. Initially, a large indoor flight, or an outside aviary, should be understocked. You can then add birds, a pair at a time, and see how well they settle in with the residents. An aviary is just like a neighborhood, but with the

The Owl Finch (*Poephila bichenovi*) is not only pleasing in appearance, but it has a delightful personality as well as a peaceful congeniality towards all other birds. It makes a wonderful addition to any aviary.

Adult pair and juvenile Gouldian Finches (*Poephila gouldiae gouldiae*). Breathtakingly beautiful, the Gouldian Finch is not recommended to beginners in the hobby. Even where all recommendations as to care and feeding have been followed, some have been known to become ill and drop over dead despite all precautions.

advantage to you that if some residents prove to be a constant source of trouble, you are able to remove and replace them with more sociable tenants!

Be aware of the fact that because two birds are of the same species it does not mean they will automatically be compatible with each other. Some will settle together right away, others after a few domestic quarrels. Others may never accept each other and will constantly fight, so must be separated. Nothing is totally predictable where birds are concerned, it being a case that you learn a little at a time by observing their habits over a period of time—which is how you become an experienced aviculturist. Before adding any birds to a collection, read up as much as you can about their known general dispositions and particular needs. If in doubt, leave them out.

CLIMATIC CONSIDERATIONS

Two aspects should be considered under this heading: where you are living and where the birds are coming from. Obviously, birds that are native to tropical countries are not going to survive if placed in outdoor aviaries in a country that experiences extremely cold winters. Some species will in fact adapt quite well to colder regions if they are acclimatized very carefully over a number of seasons—other species will never cope with frosts and low temperatures, so must always have heated winter quarters. Imported, as well as cage bred and kept birds, will always be more delicate than home bred stock that has always been accustomed to outdoor aviary life. If you plan to keep your birds in an outdoor aviary, check if the species is known to be able to cope with the winters.

SEXUAL DIMORPHISM

Sexual dimorphism means being able to distinguish the sex of a bird by its appearance. In finches and finch-like birds this is variable. In some species sexing of adults is easy, in others almost impossible, and in yet others it is only possible when the birds are in breeding condition and the cock displays nuptial (brighter-colored) plumage. Such birds are said to be in full color (IFC) as compared to their non-breeding state of out of color (OOC). Immature birds will be a much duller color than the adults. Only at this time can you be really sure of their approximate age. Full adult plumage is attained at about six months of age, though this can be at a later date if the rearing conditions have not been ideal. Once in adult plumage, this will be replaced each year shortly

Some finch species are sexually dimorphic, such as the Zebra Finch, (*Poephila castanotis*). In most color varieties, the male Zebra Finch has a large oval patch of bright rust-red bordered on the front side by a fine line of black which starts at the eye giving a tear stained effect.

The Cutthroat Finch *(Amadina fasciata)*, is so called because of the red-ribboned throat; the female lacks this and is a much duller version of the male. It is a delightful species to keep within an aviary. The males are particularly amusing because they thoroughly enjoy displaying, and they sing and dance as often as possible.

after the breeding period.

BANDING

A bird may carry one of two forms of legbands. The closed band made of metal is placed on the leg a few days after a chick is born, or a split band can be placed onto the leg, and removed, at any time. The closed band will carry a year date, as well as maybe an owner's club identification mark in the form of a sequential number. Closed bands are the only reliable means of telling the age of an adult, and they are invariably a legal requirement for birds that may be native to your country. They show that the bird was bred in captivity and not taken from the wild.

It is illegal in most western countries to take native birds from the wild, and the fines for doing so can be very high. The authorities can confiscate all such native birds you own, so check out very carefully any stock you purchase which is a native, or even migrant, resident of your country. If it carries no legband, you should not purchase it.

Some breeders of foreign species do not believe in placing bands on the legs of their birds. They fear the birds may become entangled on bushes, or the aviary netting. In such instances you can only take their word as to the given age of a specific individual. They may have placed coded split bands on young stock still in cages, and such bands are normally an acceptable guide to the age of the bird if the breeder keeps sound records.

Top: In a large collection of birds, breeders will often identify their birds by placing bands on their legs. It is easy to spot the band on the leg of this male Zebra. *Bottom:* Being small birds Finches can quickly succumb to an illness and may perish before you even know it is ill. It is therefore important that you know your stock well and respond quickly to any behavioral changes.

HEALTHY STOCK

Finches, being small birds, can quickly succumb to many avian illnesses. When they do, they may rapidly deteriorate and die. For this reason it is essential that only the healthiest birds are purchased. You do not need to be an expert to pick out healthy stock. Start by observing the conditions under which the birds are being housed. If they are packed in cages, this is a bad sign

It is easy to distinguish between the male and female Zebra Finch. Females are drab by comparison to the male, and other than lacking the orange cheek patches and bright beak, they lack the zebra markings on the chest and the chestnut and white flanks.

next step is to observe the birds. Finches are very active little creatures, so will be hopping from one perch to another, feeding, preening and generally moving about quite a bit. Any that sit hunched on their perch with their feathers fluffed up and their head drooping forward are not healthy. Any that are seen huddled in a corner of their cage are either very nervous or very ill. Sometimes recently purchased stock in a store may try to hide in a corner, but you can usually tell if their condition is due to poor health or their simply being frightened. Do not go too close to the cage initially as even an ill bird may summon up enough energy to flutter about if it is startled. Once you have spotted one or two birds that appeal to you, take a closer look at them. Their eyes should both be round and clear, with no signs of weeping. The nostrils should likewise be clear of any swellings or signs of a discharge. The beak should be neatly aligned and in no way damaged. The legs should be straight with all four toes present—three facing forwards and one backwards.

The vent area should be clean with no congealed fecal matter present, nor any undue staining of the feathers, which might suggest a recent illness. The feathers of the body should be neat and smooth, laying close to the body and suggesting good health. A missing or bent feather is not a problem as this will be replaced at the next molt. However, any bare areas clearly indicate something is amiss. Birds may be denuded of

because any bird that is ill will quickly pass its problem to all the others sharing the accommodation. The cage should be clean, as should all perches and feeding dishes. The floor should not be full of hardened fecal matter, and any blood stained feces seen is obviously a sign that one or more of the birds is ill. The selling establishment should leave you with no query as to its state of cleanliness, and if it does, you should make a rapid exit.

If the conditions satisfy you, the

head feathers by other birds out of boredom, or the head feathers of young birds may have been plucked by the hen while they were in the nest. Other than looking rather unsightly, such birds may not be unhealthy, and the feathers will be replaced in due course.

If a bird appears to have indentations on either side of its breastbone, this is not a healthy sign. It is known as "going light." It is not a condition in itself but merely a symptom of any of many problems, and is not readily corrected. Finally, where young stock is concerned, you will need the seller's assurance that the birds are feeding themselves. It is obviously better if you can see them consuming seed.

HANDLING AND TRANSPORTING BIRDS

The seller will normally catch the birds for you and place them in a small cardboard box. If you have a foreign finch showcage, this is ideal for transporting birds. Note that a budgie show cage is unsuitable because many of the smaller finches could easily escape through the wider bars of these cages. When catching a bird you simply place your hand in the cage and usher the bird to the cage bars or the floor. Then, place your hand around its body so that its head is encircled by your thumb and finger. You may, for added security, restrain its head movement by gently holding this between your thumb and finger, but be very sure you are not applying pressure.

Red-billed Firefinch, (*Lagonosticta senegala*). Finches are very delicate birds and must be handled with care. Be sure you know the proper way to handle your finch otherwise you could harm it badly.

Finches will not harm you with their beaks, which are not strong. The exception may be one or two of the larger species, such as grosbeaks and their like. These, however, do not compare with

The Painted Finch, (*Emblema picta*), is peaceful and somewhat shy in captivity. It is hardy after an acclimation period during which it is sometimes more delicate than many Australian Finches.

even the smaller of the parrot family for beak power. The use of gloves should be avoided if at all possible, because you lose the sense of touch, and may exert too much pressure on the bird, which

Facing page, lower photo and below : A male and female Purple Grenadier (*Uraeginthus ianthinogaster*). This rare species will be quite costly if found. They are fairly delicate and cannot withstand temperatures below 40° F.

will make it even more fearful of you.

Collect birds as early in the day as possible so they have time to settle into their new accommodation. On long journeys it is wise to use a more substantial container than a cardboard box. It should have the floor covered with seed. If a cage is used, remove the perches. Once you have an established collection of birds, any additional stock should be quarantined.

ACCOMMODATIONS

Compared to the parrots, finches are much easier to cater to because they are not destructive to their accommodation. Further, if the housing is to be an aviary or a large internal flight, you can also plant shrubs in this which is not possible with parrot-like birds because of their destructive habits where vegetation is concerned. Your choice of housing will be an aviary, an indoor flight, a cage, or a combination of these. You then have the option of purchasing ready-made units, or buying panels so you can design your own cage or aviary. If you are a handy person, it will obviously be less costly to build your own aviary, and this has the benefit that it can be tailored to your specific needs. The most important considerations with respect to either aviaries or cages is that they are both spacious and constructed of materials that will give you many years of wear.

AVIARIES AND INDOOR FLIGHTS

Without a doubt an aviary or a large indoor flight is easily the best way to accommodate a collection of finches. Cages are fine as a short term means of housing stock or breeding pairs, but all birds should have regular access to spacious flying areas. If not, they are leading a life of virtual imprisonment in the small confines of even a good-sized

An outdoor aviary can add to the beauty of your yard. Be sure that it is a safe structure that will supply your finches with plenty of exercise and adds to their well being.

For traveling purposes it is best to use a small box-type cage so that your birds will not injure themselves.

cage. Only if given ample room to fly can they develop the health and muscular strength that is essential to any animal, especially if it is expected to breed. An aviary may be of the ornamental type which will house a number of birds, or it can be of the design favored by most aviculturists who breed their stock which is usually a row of small flights extending from a birdroom that runs along the back of these. This provides a place for you to store food and other needed items, as well as providing a variably sized internal shelter for the birds to retreat to overnight. In the shelter their feeding dishes will be placed, as well as roosting perches.

An indoor flight is an excellent way of housing a number of finches, for it gives them much more space in which to fly. You will find great pleasure in this type of accommodation, and it can be designed to blend in with the decoration of any room. It could be placed in a garage or other outbuilding that is not being used. Before deciding on the design of your aviary or indoor flight, you are recommended to visit the aviaries of as many birdkeepers as possible. They will be happy to advise you of the relative merits of their particular layout. The various avicultural magazines often feature aviary designs, so they are worth purchasing. If you wish to build your own aviary or indoor flight, contact your local pet store for more information on this subject.

CAGES

Cage styles range from those used by exhibitors, stock cages needed in most birdrooms, and the more fancy cages sold for housing pet birds in homes. The flexibility of use. They should be covered with a non-lead paint so they can easily be wiped clean. If you make your own cages you could use one of the laminated woods, which are extremely easy to keep clean, but more costly to build. You will need to purchase finch fronts for them with narrower metal bars than are used for budgerigars, and a different door arrangement. Dowel perches are available from your pet store in range of thicknesses

Your local pet shop will be fully stocked with cages and supplies. Ask your dealer to recommend a suitable sized cage for the species you intend to keep.

first two named are made of wood while the pet bird cage is usually of chromium-plated, or epoxy resin-coated metal. Even if you do not plan to exhibit your finches, a showcage is a very handy unit. It makes an ideal transport cage for birds. Each of these cages can be purchased from your local pet store.

Stock cages can be made, or purchased in unpainted wood. They can be single, double or triple cages with removable sliding panels so they offer and shapes. Avoid those made of plastic, as they are not good for the feet of your birds.

If you are thinking of purchasing a fancy cage for your pet finches, bear in mind that length is far more important than height, though the latter should be ample. The tall, circular cages of ornate design often sold for finches are of no practical use at all to any birds. The favored shape will be a rectangle in which there is as much length as possible. If you have an alcove or similar area in your home, it is actually much better to build an internal flight cage into this as it will offer the birds a much better home—and you will enjoy watching them all the more. In such a flight you have far more scope to decorate it with natural branches than in a small cage. It will also allow you to keep more finches than will be the case even in a large stock cage.

As the aviary, indoor flight, or cage, will effectively represent the total world to your finches, it behooves you to give as much thought to it as possible. Try to give them the most spacious accommodation you can, so they can enjoy life as much as you will in watching them.

An outdoor flight cage may be of a simple design or may be quite shapely. Length and width will benefit your stock more than height, so be sure to supply your pet with plenty of room.

Do not overcrowd your aviary. Your stock will suffer from being crowded and will not retain their optimum health form being housed in such a manner.

FEEDING

It is perhaps unfortunate that the term "seed eating birds" has for so long been appended to the group of birds we refer to as finches. While it is true that for most finch species seed is in fact the basis of their diets, it has resulted in the mistaken belief by many pet owners that this is the only form of food needed by these

regions have a need for a diet that includes a variety of non seed foods.

The quantity of non-seed foods taken by finch and finch-like species will thus reflect the area of the world from which they originally came. Your finches may well be able to survive on a Spartan seed diet, but if they are

Outdoor aviaries should provide protection from the weather so that foods do not become wet and easily spoiled.

avians. Finches are found in a very extensive range of habitats that vary from desolate and barren areas of the world, to places that are rich in vegetation of all kinds. Not surprisingly, birds from extensive habitats enjoy a very varied diet that is not restricted simply to seeds. Even birds from the more desolate

to be seen at their best, and expected to breed and rear healthy clutches of chicks, it is most important that they receive a very varied diet. This diet can conveniently be divided into seed and non-seed foods.

SEEDS
The range of seeds available

Fresh vegetables, greens and fruits will be readily accepted by your finches. It will provide them with a well-balanced diet and they will not become bored with the same foods daily. This zebra finch *(Poephila guttata castanotis)* enjoys a hearty meal.

commercially for feeding to your birds is very limited when one thinks in terms of the vast number of seeds a bird may be able to select from in its natural environment. However, the seeds sold by pet stores have proven to be very acceptable to most birds kept under captive conditions. They can be divided into groups based on their nutritional content. There are seeds rich in carbohydrates, and those which have a high protein and fat content. Each type is important to the birds.

Carbohydrates are required as fuel for muscular exertions. Proteins are needed to build tissue and replace that worn out by muscular activity. Fats serve many functions in the body, as well as giving food its taste. They too can provide energy. However, as protein- and fat-rich seeds are much more costly than carbohydrate seeds, it would not be very cost-efficient to use these as a source of providing the bird's day-to-day energy needs.

The seeds given to your birds should thus reflect the time of the year, the age, and the general activity level of the birds. For example, during the breeding season pairs of birds will need extra protein seeds that will be fed to the chicks to help them develop good muscle. In the non-breeding season, the adults will not need as many protein and fat seeds. In cold climates, high fat-content

Specially designed feeders will make it easier for your finches to feed from the ground. There are many different styles and designs available from your local pet shop.

as active as aviary birds, so will not need either as much seed, nor as many protein seeds, as an aviary bird.

When feeding finches, do not ration the amount of seed supplied, because birds must always have seed available to them at all times. You should exercise selection over the types of seeds they are given, and the ratio of one to the other. It is most important that you understand that a finch has a high metabolic rate. It cannot store quantities of food in its stomach like humans and it needs to eat constantly in order to maintain its health and

The most common type of feeder is a gravity feeder. Be sure to check this daily to ensure that its openings have not become clogged.

seeds may be appreciated by the birds during the winter if they are in outdoor flights. They will help provide a layer of insulation against the cold. Such a need will not be present in pet birds kept in warm rooms, or by birds living in areas that never experience very cold temperatures.

Young birds will need a good level of protein seed, as they must build up their bodies. Likewise, birds recovering from an illness will need such seeds. While they were ill they probably did not eat much, so will have oxidized body tissue to provide energy. Such tissue must be replaced as the birds recover. In general, a pet bird confined to a cage will not be vigor. If seed is not always available, it could quickly become starved.

For those keeping only a few finches, as pets in the home, it is probably best to purchase the ready-mixed packets of seeds sold in pet stores for these birds. They are of a high quality and contain the main seeds that your pet will enjoy. The quality brands will have been fortified with vitamins and minerals. If you plan to keep

economy if it takes a long while for you to use it up. The longer it is sitting in storage, the greater the chance it could become spoiled. It is better to take a balanced view and keep about enough for one month at a time. This way you have a constant supply of fresh seed. The following are the main seeds taken by finches.

Carbohydrate-rich seeds: Various millets. These include

All finches, including Zebra Finches, readily enjoy eating millet in its natural form on the ear. Do not supply this daily as you will find your birds gorge themselves on this and ignore their daily diet.

a larger number of finches, then it will be more economical to purchase your seed in bulk quantities. Seed merchants will sell this in various finch mixtures, or you can purchase the individual seeds by the pound and make up your own mixes. Never purchase too much seed at one time, as this will prove false

Panicum, Japanese, and yellow, and white varieties. Panicum is probably the most widely used by foreign birdkeepers. It is also sold in sprays, and this form is especially enjoyed by birds. However, if they get too much of it in spray form, it may make them rather picky where other seeds are concerned, so it is best used only as a treat. Other carbohydrate-rich seeds include canary seed, wheat, and maize, although the latter two may have to be soaked in water to make them more appealing.

Protein and fat-rich seeds: Among these, the most widely used are linseed, hemp, niger, maw and rape. The latter two are especially rich in oils (fats) with a content in the order of 40%. Seed merchants will, from time to time, offer other less well-known seeds, wild plants. If you see birds in your garden pecking at certain flower heads or plants, you can be satisfied the plant is safe to give to your birds. Give them the whole plant, tied in bundles, and they will sort out what parts of it they want. However, wild plants may have been treated with pesticides, so if you are not sure on this account (as when gathering them from the countryside), it is always worthwhile to give them a rinse

Most finches enjoy a variety of seeds. As special treats you may supply them with their favorite in an extra quantity.

and it is always worthwhile trying some of these to see how your birds like them. The merchant should be able to tell you what their basic content is (i.e. if they are oil-or carbohydrate-rich seeds).

Apart from seeds obtained from pet stores, your birds will appreciate the ripening seeds of under a faucet.

A final comment on seeds is that if you take a small quantity of these and soak them in warm water for about 24 hours, this will not only soften them, but change their content value. They will invariably be appreciated by all finches in this form, and are

A good seed mixture can be purchased from your local pet store. It is easiest to purchase this in smaller quantities so that it remains fresh.

especially beneficial to young birds and those recovering from an illness. They must be well-rinsed after the period of soaking. Any seeds uneaten after a reasonable length of time should be discarded, as they will quickly deteriorate.

OTHER FOODS

Under this heading comes a large variety of items that will variably be enjoyed by your birds. The list includes fruits, wild plants, such as dandelions, shepherd's purse, chickweed, grasses and many others that may be common to your locality. Toasted bread, cereals, cookies and cakes can be crumbled and mixed, while many vegetables, such as

In the wild, birds such as the Java Rice Bird (*Padda oryzivora*) will travel far for their food to ensure variety. In captivity they cannot do so. Be sure to supply your birds with enough variety so that they do not suffer.

carrots, beets, boiled potatoes, and peas can be grated, or otherwise rendered into small pieces that a finch could swallow. You can mix all of these to form a damp salad and the birds will enjoy pecking over this.

Your pet shop will also sell soft food mixes which are rich in protein matter, such as insects, and this too will be readily taken by certain finches, less so by others. It is very nutritious, thus valuable to breeding birds. Your pet shop will also sell live foods, such as worms and assorted insects, and these are essential to most breeding finches. Of course, birds in aviaries which are planted will catch any spiders or flies that come their way. Boiled egg yolk, grated cheese, bread soaked in milk, and beef extracts, are other highly valuable sources of protein that can be offered to your birds as part of their feeding regimen. The greater the variety of foods, the more interesting the menu becomes to the birds. It also dramatically reduces the possibility that any important vitamin or mineral is lacking in the diet. Of course, water is the source of life and must be available to your birds at all times. It should be replenished every day as it quickly sours, especially in an aviary situation.

FEEDING DISHES

For those with just a few finches, it is probable that they will use one of the automatic seed and water dispensers which can be fitted to the cage bars. They come in a wide range of sizes and shapes, those with wide seed trays being preferred to tubular types with a more restricted opening. The cost of seed varieties not liked by the birds, thus thrown away, will be minimal where pet birds are concerned. However, this could be a costly loss to a breeder with many pairs, so a different approach is needed. The seed varieties are best placed

Especially where a large number of birds are owned, you should endeavor to always watch your stock at feeding times. Often, the first visible signs of an illness will be the bird's reduced interest in its food. By observing the birds you will soon get to know which are the eager feeders, the slow, and the shy ones. It is always worthwhile

All fresh greens should be thoroughly washed and free of pesticides or other harmful chemicals. Your birds will devour most greens that are offered.

in separate dishes. In this way the birds will be able to choose which seeds they want. This means you will soon have a good idea of what ratio of one seed to another your birds are taking. Open dishes should be blown over each day, otherwise it may look as if there is plenty of seed, when the reality is that there are no seeds, but a lot of husks! Automatic dispensers should be routinely tapped each day to ensure that no seeds are clogging the outlet hole.

having more than one feeding station to enable the more timid species or individuals to get their share of the food. Sometimes a greedy bird will perch close to a food dish and not allow certain other birds to approach it when they wish.

In an aviary the feeding dishes are best placed in the shelter, which will encourage the birds to use this at night. It should be mentioned that when plants in bundles are hung up in the aviary, they may not be accessible to all species. Some finches are experts at hanging on to suspended bunches of plants, others are not, and can only take them if they are either on the floor or tied to the aviary netting.

SUPPLEMENTS

If your birds are taking a well rounded diet, vitamin supplements should not be needed. An excess of vitamins and minerals can be as harmful as too little. Your guide on this matter must be the condition of the birds themselves. If you feel they could be in better health, then discuss their diet with your vet who can advise you as to what vitamins may be needed.

However, you should not forget to include grit, in the form of building rubble, rock salt, or charcoal, in your bird's diet to aid its digestion. Cuttlefish bone is also important as a source of calcium, and can be sprinkled in powder form over the bird's food.

Some breeders may use any of the coloring agents or foods now available. These may be in the form of a powder, a liquid, or a food, and are intended to improve the plumage of certain birds who lose their color in aviary conditions. However, as the use of coloring agents is generally frowned upon, I would not recommend the use of these agents to manipulate your bird's color.

The water dish that you supply for your birds will more than likely also be used as a bath. Be sure to check this daily as it can become empty after several birds have bathed.

A feeding dish should be large enough so that it allows several birds to feed from it at the same time and to avoid squabbles.

WHEN TO FEED

As already mentioned, seed and water should be available to your birds at all times, so it is a case of filling up their dishes as needed. Green and soft foods are best given early in the morning, or in the late afternoon. At these times the birds are able to consume them before the heat of the sun has had time to dry or sour them (this being especially so with bread soaked in milk). If you can arrange your schedule so that the feeding of non-seed items is at the same time each day, this will be appreciated by the birds. They will look forward to your arrival in order to see if their favorite tidbits are on that day's menu.

The feeding of finches is very straightforward, it being a case of your trying out a whole range of foods, plus their basic seeds. Remember that, like us, they are creatures of habit and tend to ignore that with which they are not familiar. This means that you may have to persevere in offering certain foods before you can be sure they just don't like it. Once one bird takes an item, the others will often follow suit. If the adults come to accept a varied diet, their chicks will do likewise, so it is a case of getting the feeding circle commenced. Never be afraid to experiment with foods. In general, you can work on the basis that if you can eat it, so can your birds—whether or not they will do so, or whether it has any great value, is another matter that only time will reveal to you.

HEALTH CARE

Finches, even the larger species, are small birds. This means they can rapidly fade away should they become unwell. A bird that is showing signs of an illness in the morning can be dead within hours. The only conclusion you can draw from this fact is that treating finches for an illness is unlikely to bring about a recovery for any but the most minor of complaints. This so, the emphasis has to be on prevention, because there will be precious little time for a cure once an illness becomes apparent. You must be ever-vigilant for the slightest change in the behavior patterns of your birds, and hygiene must be maintained to the very highest of standards.

Pet birds kept in home cages or indoor flights will be less at risk to major diseases than aviary birds. This is because they will not be exposed to quite the same factors as the latter birds. They will not have wild birds dropping fecal matter into the flight, nor will there be quite as much air movement bringing in potential pathogens. Further, there will not be as many birds being kept in a confined area.

THE PRIME REASONS FOR ILLNESS

When a bird becomes ill, this is the end result of a chain of events, not simply something that suddenly occurs. If we list the causal reasons for an illness, the following will be the ones that

Should one of your stock die for no apparent reason, it is wise to save the body and bring it to your veterinarian for a post mortem to determine the cause.

A daily bath will keep your finch's feathers healthy and clean. Be sure the bird is not placed in a draft after it has bathed otherwise it will quickly catch a chill and become sick.

most often create the problem.

1. Unclean living conditions. This will be in respect to food and water containers, perches, floors, nest boxes, and cages. Each of these represents a potential habitat for millions of pathogens (disease causing organisms). Make sure you clean all perches and food dishes daily, and cages or flights weekly. Also, don't forget to wash your hands after handling each bird.

2. Overcrowding. When too many birds are placed into a given space, this dramatically increases the chances that any one of the birds will become ill. For one thing it creates stress, and this consumes nervous energy. This lowers a bird's resistance to any illness that might come along, which under normal conditions would easily be warded off by the bird's immune system. Once one bird is ill, the illness will pass by direct or close contact. In both instances, this will obviously be more likely if many birds are living in a cramped situation.

Overcrowding means there will be a greater concentration of fecal matter lying around than there should be, and greater contamination of seed, water, and perches. Where overcrowding is seen, one usually finds lack of hygiene by the birdkeeper, because a diligent aviculturist would never allow conditions to become overcrowded in the first place.

3. Bad Food. This is linked to unclean conditions. If a birdroom

or cage is dirty, it will not take long for the food to become contaminated with pathogens. While even careful birdkeepers may occasionally supply soured or otherwise fouled food to their birds, this would normally be rare. Those who try to trim their overheads by feeding cheap seed, overripe fruit, and hastily gathered wild plants, are clearly more likely to end up with bad food than those who will only purchase fresh, quality foods.

4. Lack of Prompt Action. Many birds that could have been saved will die because the owner failed to take prompt action when necessary. Through lack of time spent with the birds, the first signs of an impending illness may not be noticed. Be especially watchful when birds are molting, as they are very vulnerable at this time. Even when illness is noticed, the owner may delay removing birds that clearly should be removed for treatment, or at least isolated observation. This lack of action places all of the other birds at risk.

5. Lack of Quarantine. There are breeders who dismiss the value of quarantine on the grounds that the recommended period of 14-21 days may not be sufficient for all illnesses to show themselves. Such an attitude is very short-sighted, because this period will reveal most diseases a bird is likely to have. It will also give the owner the opportunity to

In the wild, birds will bath from their drinking holes. This helps to keep them healthy as well as replenish fluids the hot sun takes away.

An ill finch can quickly perish. A sick bird will perch fluffed up, may have diarrhea, and will have a poor appetite.

see that the bird is eating well. A newly acquired bird that is incubating an illness will quickly pass this on to all other stock it comes into contact with if it is placed immediately into an aviary or birdroom situation. It is therefore sound husbandry to keep it away from all other stock until you are satisfied it had no major problems when you purchased it. As a routine measure, birds in quarantine can be treated for mites via any of the available aerosols. This can be repeated, as directed on the packaging, before the birds are placed within the aviaries or main birdroom. You could also treat for worms during the isolation period.

HOSPITAL CAGE

If you have more than just a few finches, a hospital cage would be a sound investment. You can purchase commercial units, or make your own. The latter is much the cheaper proposition and will do just as good a job— better in the opinion of many birdkeepers. What you will need is a wooden stock cage about 93cm

(36in) long. The internal surfaces of this should be very well-painted so they can be easily cleaned.

Two perches, quite low down, will enable the invalid to hop on and off them without too much effort. Food and water pots should be placed close to the perches. A thermometer should be placed towards one end of the cage. At that same end, an infrared lamp can be clamped to the cage bars or, better still, be free standing outside the cage. A shallow, open dish of water could be included on the cage floor in order to maintain some humidity.

If you find your finch has become ill, quickly transfer it away from all other stock and place it in an isolated cage or hospital cage. Here it can be monitored more carefully and treated on a one-on-one basis.

A thermostat should be wired into the infrared if it is not already a feature of the lamp. The temperature should be maintained at about 32°C (90°F). Having the lamp at one end of the cage enables the bird to move into a slightly cooler part if it so wishes. This will reduce the risk of it being stressed, which can be a problem with fully glass-sealed commercial cages.

It is quite amazing just how rapidly a bird will recover with no more help than heat. Broad-spectrum antibiotics can be obtained from your veterinarian and added to the drinking water. If this is done, all green foods should be withheld so the bird is more encouraged to drink water. Adding medicines to the water is not an ideal way of dosing a bird (because you cannot be sure how much it will drink) but it is often the only option. You could place powdered medicines on fruit, but the bird may not take this. Seed must always be available, though the patient may be too weak to crack this. Soaked seed or millet sprays are the obvious additions to help ensure the bird continues to eat.

In order that the bird is able to eat and drink whenever it so wishes, it is beneficial to place a low wattage, or blue, light close to the cage. This will allow the bird to see at night, without the light being so strong that it affects its

It is imperative that you check your stock daily and be able to recognize what normal behavior is so that you are aware when something is amiss. An overgrown beak may prohibit a bird from eating, and therefore this needs to be taken care of at first notice.

ability to sleep in comfort. Once a bird shows signs of recovery do not stop supplying any medicine your vet may have provided—complete the course as instructed. Once recovered, slowly reduce the heat in the cage until it is room temperature, this can be done over 3-5 days. Do not return the bird to outside aviaries if it is winter, as this might prompt a chill.

VETERINARY TREATMENT

As the reality is that few aviary owners will take their ill birds to the vet, it becomes a case of describing to him or her what the clinical signs of the illness are. In doing this you must document as much information as possible from which the vet might attempt a diagnosis. Such data as the following will be of great help.

1. How long the bird has been ill.

2. How rapidly the condition progressed.

3. How long the bird has been owned.

4. Are any others birds showing signs of the same condition?

5. What color is its fecal matter, and is this firm or liquid?

6. Is there any accumulation of rotting vegetation (grass clippings, etc.) near the aviaries?

7. What are the exact symptoms of the illness (such as the bird's state of breathing, are the eyes or nose running)?

Clearly, your vet would much prefer to see the bird and this is the best way to proceed. However, the time element involved, and the fact that you may have placed the bird in a hospital cage, or at least in a warm environment, will normally preclude transporting a finch to a veterinary clinic. Many finch owners do not bother at all with vets where illness and finches are concerned. They diagnose and treat their own birds. The high price of finches is, however, changing matters. Veterinary knowledge on birds, especially via parrots, has improved in leaps and bounds, so their advice is well-recommended these days. The available treatments for birds has likewise improved dramatically from past years.

If two or more of your birds do die, it may be a good idea to arrange for a vet to do a post mortem on them. This will identify the cause of death and enable you to save other birds.

No specific diseases and conditions have been discussed in this short chapter because of space limitations. If you wish to study avian diseases in detail you are recommended to obtain the book Bird Diseases by Arnall & Keymer, published by TFH Publications. This work covers all aspects of avian ailments.

Accumulated bird droppings can be quite messy if the perch area is not cleaned on a regular basis. Healthy birds, like the Parson Finch *(Poephila cincta cincta)* need santitary resting areas.

AVIAN CLASSIFICATION

If you are purchasing just a few finches as pets, then it is probable you will have little need to understand the basics of avian classification, unless it interests you. The more serious hobbyist will find the subject of considerable help. This is because it is an international system used by ornithologists, zoologists, and all serious aviculturists. It is the only means by which a given species can be positively identified. With over 8,500 species of birds, this need is essential.

The binomial system of nomenclature, as classification is known, is used to place all living organisms into an order of things. It enables zoologists to catalog every animal so that both individual species and whole groups of creatures can be referred to without the risk of a misunderstanding as to what group or species is under discussion. This is not possible if one uses common names. The most obvious obstacle to the use of common names is that they only hold good within a given language. Indeed, even in this they can result in confusion. For example, the Robin of England is a totally different bird to the Robin of the USA. Finches and finch-like birds fall under the order *Passeriformes.* They are then divided into families. As various groups become more and more similar, these groups are divided into genera, then into species

THE SPECIES

The species is the lowest obligate rank in any formal classification of animals. It is a collection of individuals that form a naturally interbreeding population—the word "naturally" being most important. The members of a species look very similar in appearance. However, there may be some small differences that are found regionally within a species that are consistent enough to justify their being regarded as a subspecies.

SCIENTIFIC NAMES

The scientific names of birds and other animals are written in Latin (or predominately so) because Latin was the international language of scholars, and, being a "dead" language, has the virtue of being universally accepted in all countries.

Each animal's scientific name is comprised of two parts. The first is its generic (genera) name, and the second is its trivial, or specific name. When they are combined they form the species name. The generic name always commences with a capital letter, while the trivial name always commences with a lowercase. The first of a species to be recognized is known as the nominate race. If subspecies are later discovered, then the nominate race has its trivial name repeated, thus forming a trinomial, and all the

Pintailed Parrot Finch, (*Erythrura prasina*), also known as the Pintailed Nonpareil, is the most frequently available of all the parrot finches. The greatest disadvantage to members of this family is their extreme shyness and a tendency to panic at even the most cautious approach.

other subspecies have their own unique trinom made up of the species to which their own suffix is added. For example the nominate race of the Red-cheeked Cordon Bleu is *Uraeginthus bengalus bengalus,* and one of the other four subspecies is *Uraeginthus bengalus littoralis.*

NAME CHANGES

Avian nomenclature is not a static system. It changes in order to accommodate new information on birds and the thoughts of leading experts. As a result, a bird may be taken from one genera and placed into another over a period of time. For example, Linnaeus originally placed the Red-cheeked Cordon Bleu in the genus *Fringilla,* while the Blue-headed Cordon Bleu was originally placed by Richmond into the genus *Estrilda.* Both are now together in the genus *Uraeginthus* in most modern checklists of birds. When buying finches, it is a good idea to know the scientific name of the bird you desire. This will avoid any confusion that may arise when common names differ from place to place.

The Parrot Finch has been hybridized to produce various subspecies. The Many-colored Parrot Finch *(Erythrura coloria)* is one such example.

The Parson Finch, (*Poephila cincta cincta*), is often mistaken for the Shafttail. Several features, however, are quite different: black beak instead of orange; square, short tail instead of long tapering tail; and a pale brown chest instead of soft pale gray.

The Chestnut and White Munia, (*Lonchura quinticolor*). All the birds of this genus display impeccable feathering. The birds' natural grooming does not extend to their bluish-gray feet and toenails. Heavy, unsightly scales quickly develop on feet and legs, and the toenails grow phenomenally and require frequent clipping.

A SELECTION OF SPECIES

The birds discussed in this chapter represent a selection which includes those which are inexpensive to purchase and easy to maintain, and a few which are more of a challenge to the novice. Only relatively few finches can be regarded as being easy to breed, so most of the birds featured should be given their own aviaries if it is planned to breed them. Although finches are generally very social birds there are always those who do not conform to guidelines given in books. You must therefore apply common sense judgement based on what you see happening in your aviary, rather than what books tell you should be the case!

In mixed collections start with just a few pairs or individuals, and introduce others over a period of time. This will help to ensure a harmonious situation. Finches will happily co-exist alongside certain larger birds, such as cockatiels, budgerigars, some Australian grass parakeets and most doves. However, other parrots, even small ones like the lovebirds, can be very aggressive, as can many softbilled birds. The key to how well birds can cohabit will be the size of the aviary.

Remember, if parrot—like birds are placed into a mixed collection aviary containing plants, they will quickly denude these of their leaves and flowers—which finches will not do. Try to keep the selection to species of a similar size, but of differing plumage colors. The treatment of the species is done in one of two ways. Either very popular individual species are described, or groups are discussed. The species are introduced via a few notes on their family.

Family *Emberizidae*—With about 567 species housed in five subfamilies, the emberizids represent a large and very diverse group of birds. Few of the species can be regarded as extremely popular aviary birds, and even less as typically finch-like.

The Yellow Cardinal, (*Gubernatrix cristata*), this species is probably the best breeder of the cardinal family.

Included in the family are the true buntings of the Old World, the American buntings (many of which are called sparrows or finches), the cardinals, the grosbeaks, the grassquits, and the tanagers. The latter, which comprise nearly half of the family, are regarded as softbilled birds. Only a number of the smaller species, such as the sparrows, juncos, towhees, and finches, together with the grosbeaks, are typically finch-like in that they consume a lot of seeds. Most others, including the beautiful cardinals of the USA and Mexico, require a mainly insectivorous diet if they are to be maintained in a healthy condition—and certainly if attempts are made to breed them.

Of those kept in aviculture, few are available to American birdkeepers because they are native species—but they then have the pleasure of having many of them as garden birds. In past years, a number of the species from this family, especially the cardinals, grosbeaks, the so-called finches, and the American buntings, were quite commonly available on European importers' lists. This situation has changed dramatically over recent years. These same birds have become comparatively rare. Generally, the beginner can obtain easier to manage finches from other families.

The Brazilian Crested Cardinal or Red Crested Cardinal, *Paroaria cucullata,* is the most popular cardinal in the United States. Because of its beneficial insect eating nature, it has been introduced into the Hawaiian Islands.

Black-crested finch (*Lophospingus pusillus*)— A South American bird of about 12.5cm (5in) in length. The bird is actually very pretty, and the colors attractive. Peaceful enough when not breeding, it becomes very aggressive once nesting and is best given its own quarters at this time. Not a good bird for the novice.

Saffron Finch (*Sicalis flaveola*)—This South American species of about 15cm (6in) is one of the most popular avicultural birds of this family. They are hardy birds once acclimatized and will readily breed—but will be pugnacious with smaller species. In mixed collections, keep them with Java sparrows, weavers and similar or larger birds, which are able to look after themselves. Diet is a canary mixture but live food is essential when they are breeding.

Green (Yellow) Cardinal *(Gubernatrix cristata)*— Although not the most strikingly colorful of the cardinals, this 19cm (7.5in) South American species has a good aviary record. While most cardinals will live quite well with small finches, this changes once the birds commence breeding. This species has bred well in captivity, but does need a varied live food and green food diet—which it will also take throughout the year.

Red-crested Cardinal *(Paroaria coronata)*—Another South American bird which is a long time aviary favorite. In length it is about 19cm (7.5in). It is the most popular of the cardinals in aviculture. Once acclimatized this is a hardy species, but some heat in the shelter is advised during very cold periods. Like all cardinals it enjoys picking over the ground for food. A similar bird, but lacking the red crest, is the pope cardinal, *Paroaria dominicana.*

Another popular cardinal is the Common (Virginian) Cardinal, *Cardinalis cardinalis,* which is about the same size as the previous two discussed. In captivity, the cocks often become much paler—though even in the wild there is some variation in the intensity of the red depending where the species lives.

New World Buntings (Genus *Passerina)*—Although less

The Common Cardinal, *Cardinalis cardinalis.* Like the Painted Bunting, Lazuli Bunting, and Indigo Bunting, this species cannot legally be kept in the United States.

The Painted Bunting, *Passerina ciris*, is a native to the United States and cannot legally be kept in captivity.

available than in past years, the various New World buntings are delightful species to own. Their breeding record is not good, probably because they are not supplied with the variety of insectivorous food essential to them in the breeding season. A further difficulty is the scarcity of the dull-colored hens. These birds are smaller and rather more nervous than their close relatives the grosbeaks and cardinals. In length they are all about 12.5cm (5in). The basic colors are yellow, blue, rose, and green which appear to a greater or lesser extent in five of the six species. The Indigo Bunting (*P. cyanea*) is mainly blue.

The five other species are as follows: Lazuli (*P. amoena*), Varied (*P. versicolor*), Painted or Nonpareil (*P. ciris*), Rose-bellied (*P. rositae*) and the Orange-breasted (*P. leclancherii*). The Rainbow and the Painted are probably the more popular of the group. While quite hardy, any of

the New World buntings should be supplied with some heat during very cold weather.

Family *(Fringillidae)*—This family contains the true finches of which there are about 120 species, having almost world-wide distribution. Only a few can be considered popular cage and aviary birds, but one of these, the canary, is bred in more varieties than any other pet bird. They are essentially seedeaters, but all will appreciate both green and live foods during the breeding season. A number are very modestly priced and the cocks make nice songbirds in a mixed collection. Remember that many true finches are native to both Britain and the USA, where they are protected species.

Canary *(Serinus canaria)*—Thought to have been developed from the wild canary of the

The Lazuli Bunting, *Passerina amoena*, is a very popular species in Europe. It is difficult to breed and not quite so hardy as the Indigo Bunting.

islands of that name, as well as the Azores, this is a wholly domesticated species. Size ranges from 10cm (4in) to 23cm (9in), while the body shape is equally variable from the pretty to the rather grotesque. Colors include red, yellow, green, brown, white, silver, and a host of pastel shades of these. While all cock canaries have a sweet and melodious voice, that of the roller excels all others. Prices range from very modest for pet quality to highly expensive for good show stock.

They are very social birds, so are fine for either a colony or a mixed aviary, providing they have ample territory when breeding.

There are many specialized soft and coloring foods produced for these birds. If you plan to keep them in an aviary, then endeavor to purchase hardy aviary-bred birds rather than those from

The Rainbow Bunting, *Passerina leclancheri*, is an exceptionally pretty bird, but the female is very dull by comparison.

The Indigo Bunting, *Passerina cyanea*, is a wonderful aviary bird because of its calm demeanor.

cages. They make an ideal introductory bird to the finch group. The sexes are similar in appearance.

Green (Yellow-fronted) Singing Finch *(Serinus mozambicus)*— This delightful little bird from Africa has long been an aviary favorite. While its song is not quite as sweet as its close relative the Gray (White-rumped) Singing Finch (*Serinus leucopygius*) it compensates by having more colorful plumage. Its length is about 12.5cm (5in). The hen is a duller version of the cock.

Although still modest in price, the species has increased more so than some of the other popular little finches. When breeding these birds they are best housed on their own, as they are as energetic at defending their territory as they are at singing. They have a reliable breeding record, and one for longevity. They may live to 20 years of age, an excellent lifespan for such a little bird. They can be a little

The European Serin, *Serinus serinus*, is one of Europe's favorite singing finches. Not endowed with a particularly attractive color scheme, this small songbird has a cheerful song and a pleasant disposition.

The Green Singing Finch, *Serinus mozambicus*, is a better breeder than the average waxbill but they show slight aggressiveness during the breeding season.

bossy in a mixed collection and though they will not actually harm other birds, they should be watched because they may upset more placid species. A well-recommended finch, as is the Gray Singing Finch. They are hardy and will winter without heat if the shelter is draftproof.

Greenfinch *(Carduelis chloris)*—This is a hardy aviary bird of about 15cm (6in) in length. It has a powerful beak so is not the ideal bird for mixing with small finches, though is quite sociable with those of its own size. It is a reliable breeder, and a few color mutations have been established, including the lutino, but these would be rather costly. Its song is pleasing and it

The European Goldfinch, *Carduelis carduelis britannica*, is one of the truly delightful birds of the entire world. It is very pretty, hardy, a fine songster, and a reasonably good breeder.

can be recommended to the novice. Feed a mixed-seed diet, to include larger seeds such as peanuts and sunflower, as well as green and soft foods.

Within the genus there are a number of other greenfinches, and all make interesting birds and have much the same needs. Their availability is, however, less reliable than that of the European species described, which are well-established in captivity.

Goldfinch *(Carduelis carduelis)*—The goldfinch has some twelve subspecies which are distributed from Britain and mainland Europe through Egypt, India, and as far as Siberia. It is a strikingly colorful bird of red, white, black, brown and yellow. It has a length of about 12.5cm (5in). Goldfinches are very popular avicultural subjects and are reliable breeders. They enjoy a mixed seed diet and are especially fond of the flowering heads of many wild plants such as dandelions. They can be bred in a mixed aviary, or in small colonies, so are ideal subjects for the specialist. The hens are somewhat duller than the cocks but not always.

Goldfinches will hybridize with canaries, greenfinches, and some siskins to produce beautiful and colorful birds with equally enchanting singing abilities. Be sure any youngsters that are purchased carry closed legbands as these are a protected species.

Bullfinch *(Pyrrhula pyrrhula)*—This is one of six bullfinch species that have an extensive range of distribution from Britain to Siberia, and the Azores to India and Japan. It is a large finch reaching 19cm (7.5in) so is best kept with birds of similar size. It is a hardy species not needing heating during the winter—but a draftproof shelter is recommended. It may denude shrubs of their buds and it is especially fond of various wild berries. Bullfinches are often hybridized with canaries to produce what are called mules. These are good-looking finches with the singing ability of the canary. When breeding, give them their own quarters as they are rather territorial, and will quickly squabble with their own kind. Bullfinches are very impressive exhibition birds, but such stock would be costly.

Family *(Estrildidae)*—Although this family contains only about 132 species spread across 29 genera it is, nonetheless, the family from which most popular avicultural and cage birds are derived. This is not pure chance. The various species have many advantages that have made them the mainstay of foreign birdkeeping.

1. They are small finches, few being greater than 12.5cm (5in) in length.

2. Many are very colorful.

3. All are essentially seedeaters, so are not difficult to cater to (though green and live foods are appreciated, especially in the breeding season).

4. A number have very good breeding records in captivity.

5. All are Old World species, so there are no major problems (legislation) in keeping them in the USA and Europe.

6. Many are the most inexpensive of foreign birds available to aviculture. This situation is, however, changing as more countries place restrictions on the export of their indigenous species.

7. Most are gregarious by nature and make ideal birds for either mixed or colony collections, as well as for cage breeding.

8. A few have established color mutations in them.

9. They make very attractive birds for those wishing to involve themselves in the exhibition side of the hobby.

The general ethological features of the family are as follows:

1. They form strong pair bonds.

2. Both parents share incubation duties.

3. Both parents feed the chicks.

4. Both parents help build the nest, though normally only the cock gathers the material for this.

5. The female solicits copulation by spreading her tail and rapidly quivering this.

6. Many species will roost in the nest out of the breeding season.

7. The incubation period is 12-14 days and the chicks fledge, on average, from 18-20 days. They are usually fully independent about 12-16 days later.

Within the family are the waxbills, the twinspots, the

Peter's Twinspot, *Hypargos niveoguttatus,* is said to be an excellent aviary subject and very hardy.

Australian grassfinches, the mannikins, the fire finches, the cordon bleus, the parrot finches, the silverbills, the Java sparrows and others. All are household foreign finch names that you will see in your local pet store. Prices will range from a few dollars to over a hundred, depending on the species.

The Twinspots—There are six species of twinspots housed in four genera. They cannot be considered a beginner's bird, but will be seen from time to time in pet shops.

Peter's Twinspot (*Hypargos niveoguttatus*)—is popular within the framework that none of these species are common. The species

Pair of Green Twinspots, *Mandingoa nitidula*. The entire family of Twinspots is quite similar to the Pytilias. The size and shape of their bodies is similar, their diet is equally insectivorous, and their beaks are similarly shaped.

Black-bellied Firefinch, *Lagonosticta rara* **or** *Estrilda rara*. **Firefinches are probably the best breeders in the waxbill family. Their incubation period is usually 12 or 14 days, and the young leave the nest anywhere between 17 an 21 days.**

will need heated quarters in the winter, as they are rather delicate birds even after being acclimatized. They are not prolific breeders and as they are not imported in great numbers from their African home, they will be rather costly to obtain. The same remarks apply to Dybowski's Twinspot (*Euschistospiza dybowskii*) and to the Green-backed Twinspot (*Mandingoa nitidula*), two other species sometimes offered for sale.

Senegal Fire Finch (*Lagonosticta senegala*)—This little African finch is well-recommended to the novice. It is inexpensive, colorful, a reliable breeder and, like all fire finches, makes a peaceful aviary resident.

It will tolerate others of its own and related species, so all in all has many virtues. It is about 11.5cm (4.5in) in length. With a few white spots on the body it bears a superficial resemblance to the much more costly twinspots! Fire finches need very careful acclimatization and care during their first winter, but thereafter are very hardy birds. However, it would still be prudent to supply basic heat in very cold weather.

It may be difficult to obtain pairs of fire finch species because the hens of some species often look similar and are imported in mixed batches. There are ten fire finch species and all have red as

The Red-billed Firefinch, *Lagonosticta senegala*, is extremely delicate until it is acclimated. After that period it becomes very hardy.

The Cordon Bleu, *Uraeginthus bengalus*, is one of the few finches with a beautiful shade of sky blue. Their shape is gracefully simple and seems designed for its highly active but peaceful nature.

their basic color. The Senegal is the most readily available.

Cordon Bleus (Genus *Uraeginthus*)—The three species of these birds are also known as Blue Waxbills on account of the blue areas in the plumage. They are long established aviary favorites and are bred in reasonable numbers. They are hardy birds, but some winter heating is advised. The importance of green and live foods should never be underestimated with these and most other finches. The Blue-headed Cordon Bleu, *U. cyanocephala*, is possibly the freer breeder of the trio. The other two species are the Red-cheeked, *U. bengalus*, and the Cordon Bleu, *U. angolensis*, which lacks both the bluecap and the red cheeks. Acclimatize imported birds with great care, as the quarantine period they will have gone through will not make them hardy, as is sometimes thought.

In the same genus as the cordons are the Common (Violet-eared Waxbill) and Purple Grenadiers, *U. granatina* and *U. ianthinogaster*. These are gorgeous-looking birds with splashes of violet and deep blue in the plumage, but they are expensive and not especially social in mixed collections. They

The Violet Eared Waxbill, *Granatina granatina*, is a close rival of the Lady Gouldian Finch as far as beauty is concerned. Though far less flamboyant than the Lady Gould, the Violet Eared shows a rich glow and intensity of shading which is really quite indescribable.

The Black-cheeked Waxbill, *Estrilda erythronotos*, is not considered a good breeder. Its shyness entitles it to an aviary by itself.

are also much more delicate in cold weather.

Popular Waxbills (Genus *Estrilda*)—This genus contain 16 species of little finches from various parts of Africa. They are variably available at prices from very modest to quite expensive. Without being vividly colorful they are pleasing, and are nearly always featured in mixed finch collections. Generally hardy, you must always link common sense to this term. Being little birds, they can quickly burn up energy just keeping warm, so background heat is recommended during the winter.

The Lavender Finch or Waxbill, *E. caerulescens*, is a lavender-gray color with a red rump and tail. It is a reliable breeder if it is in hardy condition. It will need an insectivorous diet during the breeding period. As with most species of the genus, the sexes are similar, so your first problem will be in obtaining a true pair. When confined to a cage for any length of time, these birds may resort to feather plucking.

Orange-cheeked Waxbills, *Estrilda melpoda melpoda*, are a favorite among beginners. They are very attractive, inexpensive, and quite hardy.

The Orange-cheeked Waxbill, *E. melpoda*, is one of the least expensive of all foreign birds. It is only 10cm (4in) in length. Although it is bred in captivity this is only on a small scale, but this could change one day. It is a timid little finch so prefers plenty of cover in an aviary.

The St. Helena (Common) Waxbill, *E. astrid*, has been popular for decades. It is arguably one of the easiest of the non-domesticated finches to cater to, and is a reliable breeder as well. You may see a few other members of the *Estrilda* genus offered for sale and most are, like the three discussed, lively little birds of reasonably hardy dispositions.

Gold-breasted Waxbill, *Estrilda subflava subflava*, is the smallest of Africa's waxbills and is as variable as a desert sunset. No two males are exactly alike in the red and red-orange shadings of the chests.

Avadavats (Genus *Amandava)*—There are three species in this genus, two being Asiatic, and one African in distribution. They are long time aviary favorites, two of them being colorful and easy to cater to. The Green Avadavat, *A. formosa*, while very pretty, is not commonly available and is the more difficult to maintain and breed.

The Red Avadavat, *A. amandava*, also known as the Red Munia, Bombay Avadavat, and the Tiger Finch, is from Pakistan and India. The cock exhibits nuptial plumage which is red on the head, the underparts and rump, the rest of the body being brown. If kept in cages, these birds may become almost

Red Avadavat, *Amandava amandava*, is unusual in that it has a seasonal change of plumage. Outside the breeding season, it may be difficult to distinguish the out-of-color male from the hen.

The Orange-cheeked Waxbill, *Estrilda melpoda*, is a very fast flyer as well as being constantly active; and it, therefore, is a vivacious addition to any collection.

The Zebra Finch, *Poephila castanotis,* is the most popular and readily available Australian finch. It is quite accustomed to living in smaller cages and breeds easily.

long-lived. Highly recommended, every beginner should own a few pairs of these birds, which will mix well with other finches in a community aviary.

Australian Grass Finches— There are about eighteen indigenous finches in Australia, and all are prized cage and aviary birds. As exports from that country are banned, all of the species seen in aviculture have been bred in captivity. With the exception of the highly popular, and now domesticated, Zebra Finch, all Australian finches will be costly, some especially so. They are not considered to be suitable birds for beginners, but the breeding record of most is far superior to that of many African and Asiatic birds that are considered ideal for the novice.

The colors seen in this group of birds ranges from pleasant to quite breathtaking. If you purchase any other than the Zebra Finch, be sure to check under what conditions the birds have been kept, because cage-bred birds will not be as hardy as those from aviaries and would need acclimatizing to such.

Zebra Finch *(Poephila guttata)*—This highly popular finch has introduced many a birdkeeper to aviculture. So available is it that its cost in its wild or normal form (wild meaning its natural coloration) is the lowest of any bird species due to the vast numbers bred. There are many color mutations, and even crested varieties. These will be more costly. The Zebra Finch is a very popular exhibition bird

black in color, but this is only temporary and will change once placed into an aviary flight for a season. The Red Avadavat has an excellent breeding record and makes a good species for the beginner. The subspecies *A. a. punicea*, is often sold as the Strawberry Finch.

The Gold-breasted Waxbill, *A. subflava*, also known as the Zebra or Orange-breasted Waxbill, is from Africa. It has always been a popular cage and aviary bird. At 9cm (3in) it is one of the tiniest of finches and is a truly delightful species to own. The species is a ready breeder, hardy once acclimatized, and

Of all the finch species, the Lady Gouldian, *Poephila gouldiae gouldiae,* **requires the warmest temperatures for good health.**

and a very good species for a mixed collection. Needless to say it is an ideal beginner's bird. It is often willing to incubate the eggs of other species, and in the process might upset more timid birds, so bear this overzealous aspect of its nature in mind.

Bicheno Finch *(Poephila bichenovi)*—In contrast to the Zebra Finch, the cute-looking Bicheno, Owl, or Double-barred Finch, is very expensive. It is also much less hardy where cold weather is concerned. Like the Zebra, it is gregarious by nature, so is quite happy in small colonies or mixed collections. It is an enchanting species that is

perhaps best obtained after experience has been gained with more popular birds.

Gouldian Finch *(Chloebia gouldiae)*—Without a doubt this is one of the most colorful of any bird species and always attracts attention when seen for the first time. Gouldians are expensive birds, and even more so for the white-breasted, and blue mutations. They need heated quarters as they do not tolerate cold temperatures at all. They are very sociable birds that can be colony-bred. Soaked seeds and soft foods are essential to Gouldians in the breeding season. Like the Bicheno, they

The Owl Finch, *Poephila bichenovi*, is a fairly long lived bird, but is not too free a breeder under captive conditions. In the wild it breeds quite readily.

Gouldian Finch, *Poephila gouldiae gouldiae*, the male of this species is the more beautiful sex. Females are duller and paler additions of the male particularly in regard to the greatly reduced intensity of the chest.

Above: African Silverbill, *Lonchura cantans*. Although rather plain colored, this little finch makes a first class addition to the mixed aviary. Below: The Bronze Mannikin, *Lonchura cucullatus*, is a hardy bird that is usually available at a very reasonable price.

are a species that the novice should aspire to own only when experience has been gained with more hardy and less costly birds.

Silverbills (Genus *Lonchura*)— There are three silverbills from which you might choose. Two are African and one is Asiatic. The silverbills are hardy and sociable birds, as well as being among the least expensive of any foreign finches. They breed well in aviaries, so are invariably among the first birds beginners will own. The sexes are similar, so it is best to purchase a trio or more in the hopes that a true pair will be among these.

The most commonly available is the African Silverbill, *L. cantans*. It is distinguished from its Asiatic form by having a dark rump whereas that of the Indian Silverbill, *L. malabarica*, is white. The Gray-headed Silverbill, *L. griseicapilla*, with white spots on the head is possibly the most attractive of the trio. However, it prefers some live foods in its breeding diet, so is a little more difficult to cater to—the other two being happy with just soft foods added to their seed rations.

The Mannikins (Genus *Lonchura*)—There are a number of mannikins which are very popular aviary birds. Certain species are also commonly seen on lists as Nuns, Spice birds, or Munias. Black, brown, and white (cream) are the predominate colors. They are generally hardy birds once acclimatized, and are also easy to cater to when breeding. At this time they will manage on a varied seed diet plus green foods and soaked seed—live food not being essential to most species, though it is always recommended for the best results. The sexes are not dimorphic, so it is a case of obtaining a number of birds and hoping pairs are found. The following are a few of the species you are likely to see in pet stores.

1. Black-headed Nun or Mannikin, *L. malacca atricapilla.* The head, throat and neck are black, the body a chestnut brown.

2. Tri-colored Nun, *L. malacca malacca.* Similar to *L. m. atricapilla* but with white underparts.

3. White- headed Nun, *L. maja.* The head, throat and neck are white, the body chestnut brown.

4. Spice Bird or Nutmeg Mannikin, *L. punctulata.* Head, throat and neck are brown, the underparts are white with a dark brown scalloped edging to the feathers.

Bengalese Finch *(Lonchura domestica)*—This bird is thought to be the domesticated form of *L. striata.* It is an extremely popular little finch that is easy to care for and a prolific breeder often used to foster the chicks of other species. The sexes are similar, but as in most of the genera, the cock will sing to the hen at breeding times, which is one way of identifying them. Bengalese are suited to either cage or aviary breeding and they will mix happily with any other small finches. Highly recommended.

Java Sparrow *(Padda oryzivora)*—This is a long time

Above: Black-hooded Nun, *Lonchura ferruginosa.* Sexing of this species is very difficult. In the extremes, males have larger and more masculine beaks than females. Most are, unfortunately, in the in-between category which makes detection impossible. Below: Tri-colored Nun, *Lonchura malacca.* The Nuns rarely rear young in captivity and determining the sex of the birds is very difficult. Behavior is a sure sign. The male sings poorly and dances comically to the hen.

Above: The Spice Finch, *Lonchura punctulata*, is not at all a ready breeder in captivity. It is a quiet bird that can be associated with any small finch provided it is not over crowded. Below: The White-headed Nun, *Lonchura maja*, is much easier to sex than the Tri-colored Nun or the Black-hooded Nun because females have a dull, dusty appearance on the white head.

aviary favorite sometimes called the Paddy Rice Bird due to its habit of feeding in rice fields in its Asiatic homelands. The Java's plumage always looks immaculate. There are established white, pied and fawn mutations, making the Java a very popular exhibition prospect. They are hardy birds that are able to look after themselves in mixed aviaries containing larger finches, or those which include weavers (which can be rather aggressive to many small finches). It is best not to include small waxbills with the Java Sparrow unless the aviary is very large and well-planted. Imported birds can prove difficult to breed, but the mutational forms are more willing. Seed (including rice), green food and soft food should be supplied. Javas are modestly priced birds.

Cutthroat *(Amadina fasciata)*—The cutthroat is so named for the red patch on the throat of the cock—this is lacking in the hen. They are also called ribbon finches. Though not the most colorful of birds, these African finches are very popular because they are easily cared for, good mixers with birds of their own size (12.5cm - 5in), and they are among the least costly of any foreign bird species. They breed readily, but at such times they can be aggressive and should not be included with small waxbills. Java sparrows, small weavers, cockatiels, and small doves are the sort of birds that are safe with cutthroats in a mixed collection.

Family *Ploceidae*—This family contains some 158 Old World species housed in 22 genera. Many members of the family are popular avicultural subjects, but most are difficult to breed. Many are parasitic on other birds (such as small waxbills). This term means that they lay their eggs in the nests of the waxbills, which then rear them. The chicks of the waxbills may be thrown out of the nest by the larger chicks of the parasitic species, or both may be reared. The aviary birds in the family include the whydahs, the weavers, and the sparrows. They tend to be rather assertive birds, so most small finches are best not housed with them. This so, they are not covered individually in this text, other than via brief mention of those most commonly seen.

Of the species that are popular in aviculture, most display nuptial plumage, so the cocks are extremely attractive when in breeding condition. When out of color (OOC) they resemble the hens, so are invariably rather drab-looking birds. In price they range from relatively inexpensive to very costly. All will be benefit from live and soft food, as well as their normal seed diet.

Pin-tailed Whydah *(Vidua macroura)*—Length 12.5cm (5in), but the cock's breeding tail feathers can be of 25cm (10in). Only house one male with a number of females.

Queen Whydah *(Vidua regia)*— Length 12.5cm (5in), but the cock may sport a tail of 20cm (8in) when in breeding plumage.

Above: Society Finches, *Lonchura domestica*. No two Society Finches are exactly alike in their mottled pattern. Coloring varies from pure white to dark chocolate brown. Below: Java Rice Birds, *Padda oryzivora*, are quite aggressive when kept among birds of other species, it is recommended that one pair be kept with other birds of the same size for breeding purposes.

Above: The nests constructed of interwoven grasses are the basis for calling the birds "weavers." Below: Napoleon Weaver, *Euplectes afra afra*. The sexes of the weavers are extremely difficult to determine while males are out of color. In nuptial display, the nape feathers are somewhat erectile.

Senegal Combassou *(Vidua chalybeata)*—Length 11.5cm (4.5in). Also called the Indigo Bird. Cock a blue-black when in color. Hen brownish above and white underparts.

Napoleon Weaver *(Euplectes afra)*—Length 12.5cm (5in). Also called the Yellow Bishop. As with others in this family, they should only be kept with other self-assertive birds in a mixed aviary situation—Java sparrows, cutthroats, budgies and their like, all of whom will stand up to them if they attempt to be too bossy.

Orange Bishop *(Euplectes orix)*—Length 12.5cm (5in). The cock in nuptial plumage is a gorgeous finch. The feathers of the neck fluff out to give the bishop's look to the bird. Like the others of this genus, the bishops are polygamous and a cock is best housed with a number of hens. A single hen might be continually harassed by a cock. Out of color, the males resemble the hens—a dull yellow-brown color.

When thinking of mixing weavers and whydahs together, bear in mind their territorial aggressive attitude during breeding periods. Avoid choosing species of similar colors. However, if breeding is attempted, it is better to give pairs, or groups, their own accommodation. Where parasitic whydahs are concerned it is essential that their host species is present in a breeding state.